Second Crop

John Sterling Harris

Second Crop

Poems by John Sterling Harris

With a Foreword by Richard H. Cracroft

BYU Studies
Provo, Utah
and
Charles Redd Center for Western Studies
Provo, Utah

BYU Studies publishes a quarterly journal and a series of monographs. For information about subscribing to *BYU Studies,* a quarterly multidisciplinary LDS journal with poetry in each issue, write to 403 CB, Brigham Young University, Provo, Utah 84602. BYU Studies and the Charles Redd Center for Western Studies gratefully acknowledge the support of BYU Scholarly Publications in making this volume possible.

The publishers of *Tar River Poetry* have generously given permission to use "Desert," "I Find Green," and "Soldiers of the Legion." See the bibliography for complete bibliographic information.

Library of Congress Cataloging-in-Publication Data

Harris, John Sterling, 1929–
    Second crop : poems / by John Sterling Harris ; with a foreword by
Richard H. Cracroft.
      p. cm. — (BYU Studies monographs)
    Includes bibliographical references.
    ISBN 0-8425-2335-9
    I. Title. II. Series.
PS3558.A6464S43 1996
811'.54—dc20
                                        96-10029
                                            CIP

Printed in the United States of America
10 9 8 7 6 5 4 3 2 1

Contents

Foreword

In *Second Crop,* John Sterling Harris presents the poetic gleanings of the two decades since he harvested his first crop of poems in *Barbed Wire* (1974; reprinted 1993). This bounteous collection nails securely to the fence post the signboard (complete with standard .22 slug holes) declaring, "John Sterling Harris, Chief Word-Wrangler among Poets of Western America." He is that, and more. As you are about to discover, if you haven't read him before, Harris is the best poet of the contemporary West.

Second Crop corrals tight, well-crafted, masculine images that soar wonderfully from precisely described earthbound objects to timeless human meanings. Like Robert Frost's, each of Harris's poems "begins in delight and ends in wisdom."[1] The pattern holds: Harris dramatizes intense, focused moments of insight as they unfold amidst the stark, strange contrasts of Utah deserts and mountains, especially the Stansbury and Oquirrh ranges.

This "type and shadow" metaphysical dynamic of Harris's poetry reflects the analogical world view of his Latter-day Saint faith, which proclaims that "all things . . . are spiritual." It also draws upon the Transcendental dualism of Emerson and Thoreau, whom he has admired and taught as a professor of literature and technical writing at Brigham Young University from 1962 to 1993. His commonplace images, from hayracks, barbed wire, and single-action Colt revolvers to Utah barns,[2] rattlers, and irrigation ditches, form the solid platforms from which Harris launches his poetic probes. They push at the edges of knowledge, enabling a sense of discovery, direction, and cosmic order in a Higher Reality that is, as he implies in "Downhill," beyond the need for eyes. Such satisfying resolution, currently called *closure,* is seldom found in contemporary minimalist poetry.

To the complex of impulses that shape Harris's poetry, one must add his comic sense, manifested in his witty wordplay; his lifelong engagement with American literature; his astonishing memory for bric-a-brac, from nuts and bolts to cabbages and kings; and his years as a by-the-numbers U.S. Army sergeant (he can break down and repair an M1 rifle—blindfolded—in record time). To understand Harris, however, one must appreciate his insatiable scientific curiosity about How Things Work. A renowned teacher of technical writing, Harris is a thorough-going scientist, and has, through several books, numerous articles, and visiting professorships, preached the gospel of tech writing across the land. He weaves literature and technology into a seamless and mutually complementary relationship, teaching tech writing like a poet and poetry like a tech writer. This unusual, yet felicitous, juxtaposition of divergent world views explains the precise, technical, stick-to-the-blueprint Things and Objects that ground his poetry, as well as the multilayered complex of meanings that the poet evokes in the reader.

Typical of Harris's dualistic poetics is the poem "E. H. 1817." In a simply, but carefully, described carpenter's framing square ("Twenty-four inches on the stock / Sixteen on the leg") used by his Mormon forefathers and inscribed "E. H. 1817," Harris reads the parallel epic stages in the build-and-flee-and-build-again history of Mormonism and the devoted Harris family. While the tech writer describes the heirloom square as an accurate instrument, still true angled and at the ready, the poet triggers emotions and the spiritual truth inherent in the simple square ("If it were needed for building / A New Jerusalem").

A final ingredient in the rich combination that is John Sterling Harris has been introduced only recently: his courageous struggle against the unrelenting chronic pain he has suffered since crash-landing his homebuilt airplane in 1989 (after several years of flying the craft not without incident, but at least without injury. Then the plane had that fateful, clogged fuel line). Harris's more-than-a-brush with death and his continuing, determined struggle to walk, write, and teach again (he taught a graduate seminar in his hospital room) have given his life an unexpected turn. (He now dates his life "B.C. and A.D.—Before Crash and After Disability"). This accident left his body badly broken, scarred, hurting, and cane-dependent—yet strengthened his character, deepened his wisdom, broadened his vista, and intensified his metaphorical vision of the world. He hints at these confrontations in "The World of Men" section, rejoicing in one poem at the freedom of "Flight" and respectfully bargaining with Death in "Disclaimer":

> Death, old friend,
> We've met before.
> I know that dour face. . . .
>
> But I'll remain a while,
> If you'll allow.
>
> For roads and tasks—
> And words not written down.
> I need not have them all,
> But some are dear.

John Sterling Harris's ripened *Second Crop,* along with a forthcoming companion volume of personal essays, *Knowing Things Together,* are my friend's moving and powerful late harvest that Death, relenting, allowed. There are many books of poetry, "but [only] some," like the one you are about to enjoy, "are dear."

RICHARD H. CRACROFT
Professor of English and
Western American Studies
Brigham Young University

Notes

¹ Robert Frost, *The Complete Poems of Robert Frost* (New York: Henry Holt, 1949), vi.

² Harris built the barn whose weathered boards you can see in the frontispiece and endpapers of this book.

Introduction

My father never got over growing up on the frontier of Chihuahua, Alberta, and Montana. He died at ninety-three, and almost his last words were, "If I could just have one more ride on old Rocko." Rocko was the big red sorrel thoroughbred he'd owned forty years before. And I have not gotten over growing up in Tooele, Utah. I left there nearly fifty years ago, but the memories of that boyhood are clear.

Beginning college students are often asked to write of their experiences, and they protest that they have not had any experience yet. If I had been given such an assignment when I entered college at seventeen, I would have made the same protest. I would have been wrong. I'd had the experience, but I could not then see that the experience was significant.

My childhood and youth were full of horses and dogs and excursions to the mountains and the desert. Sometimes I was with my father, but I was often alone, too. Like him I had a restless need to see what was on the other side of the ridge. It was not a need to glance at far places, but a need to look carefully at near places repeatedly at a different time of day or in a different season or from another direction. I do not know what I was looking for, but somehow I think that I found it. Many of these poems came out of that childhood and youth, and they are of emotion recollected not in tranquillity—I am too restless to be tranquil—but with a recognition and understanding that I hope is mature.

So most of the poems here are about that West where I grew up in a small town. Some are set in the high, craggy mountains that I traveled on horseback and afoot. In Utah the mountains catch the snowstorms and the few rainstorms, then hold the water and release it a little at a time in the creeks. These creeks—pronounced *cricks*—make life in the desert valleys possible.

A larger number of the poems are set in the west desert, a dry, dusty world out toward the Nevada line. Outlanders find that barrenness frightening. It is hard, but not malicious, and though it can be very unforgiving to anyone who goes into it unprepared, it has a harsh beauty when you come to know it well.

And I have consciously and unconsciously echoed the quiet and laconic speech of the horsemen of my youth. There were the Stookey brothers, the Warburtons, Mutt and Snub Rydalch, Ed Gillespie, Rick Dodds, Frank Durfey, and a host of others—including my uncle Leo, a Montana rancher. Their very names evoke a world of horses as well as the wild country that they loved and tried to hang on to. I, too, am reluctant to let it go.

There were other forceful memories of my youth. I have always been curious about how things were made and how they worked, and that curiosity has produced poems, too. I worked as a smelterman and as a steelrigger, and for myself and for my employers, I built structures and machines. There is much that is poetic in anything well made.

When I left Tooele, I became a student, a missionary, a soldier, and a professor. And I built, flew—and eventually crashed—a two-hundred-mile-an-hour experimental airplane. In these other lives, though the artifacts and venues changed, I found myself repeating the lessons I had learned as a boy.

Hawthorne, in one of his notebooks, said something like "A beam of light passing through an imperfect blind into a darkened room, falls upon an open book. It might be made symbolical—of something." I have found many things in the West that shout to be seen as symbolical.

But poems are not just subject matter. Hawthorne's contemporary, Emerson, said that "poetry is Nature passed through the alembic [the distilling apparatus] of man." But each person—or alembic—is different, and some of that change in Nature—or the thing that might be made symbolic or just remarkable—is distilled by that person's conscious or subconscious character. Other changes are wrought by the poet as craftsman.

I spent most of my life as a technical writer and teacher of technical writing. I edited a couple of books on geology and wrote many articles on aircraft design and on firearms technology. And I wrote three books and innumerable articles on technical writing. These experiences have occasionally been subject for poetry, but even more they have been the source of the method of my poetry.

As I have written at length elsewhere, the scientist, engineer, or technical writer makes frequent use of the scientific model—a comparison in words or equations that helps explain and predict the behavior of the physical world. The poetic metaphor is another name for this kind of modeling. Scientific and technical things are appropriate subjects for poetry—we do not have to confine ourselves to bluebirds and daffodils; we can write of entropy and hand grenades, too. Technical writing shares with poetry a need for precision in diction and a need for economy—always economy—in style. The forms of technical writing—mechanism description, process description, definition, classification, and interpretation—are also appropriate forms for poetry.

Elmer Keith, after a long and adventurous life, wrote an autobiography with the felicitous title *Hell, I Was There.* I believe that for a novel, poem, play, or history to be any good, it must deserve *Hell, I Was There* as a subtitle. The author must speak with the convincing authority of one who has in some fashion been there. And that authority must be based on a truth that may go beyond mere fact. I can tolerate convincing invention or outright lies, but I cannot abide inaccuracy. I once included in a poem the line "And eagles with their bowed and tilting wings." On closer examination, I had to make it "condors with their bowed and tilting wings." I wanted the image of bowed wings, but soaring eagles' wings are straight out! That was probably the technical writer editing the poet.

The poet and the technical writer are in conflict in other ways. The technical writer is obsessed with clarity. Clarity never faileth. The poet delights in ambiguity and multiple levels of meaning. This difference provides difficult choices. I try to achieve clarity at one level and let additional levels occur as they can. When the subject matter is likely to be unfamiliar to the reader—some of my readers are culturally deprived from not having grown up in rural Utah—I try to explain my subject within the poem, but too much explanation can ruin a poem. So when the explanation would unduly interrupt or cannot be easily looked up, I have in a few cases, cheated by providing notes. You are welcome to use the notes or ignore them and find your own solutions.

When poetry is written by the conscious and informed by the subconscious, the old English teacher's question invariably comes up "How much did the poet intend?" Was that additional meaning intentionally placed or not? My subconscious has an answer to these questions. If you found a level of meaning or a connection that gave you pleasure, I intended it. If you didn't like the level or connection, then maybe not.

> The poet from himself
> And his cosmos
> Forges an anvil
> Ironically
> According to his cast
> And his temper
> Then grinds it hard
> And files it.
>
> Upon its polished face
> He lays his reputation
> And his gonads
> Handing hammers out to all
> Inviting them to swing
> And prove his metal.

Note

Related essays—"West Desert," "The Love of Machines," and "Poetry and Technical Writing"—are in *Knowing Things Together* (Provo, Utah: BYU Studies, forthcoming in 1996).

West

Rattler

I saw him there beside the road,
Coiled as if waiting to strike, but still,
And with head unaccountably low.
As I approached,
I heard no buzz of rattles,
But saw the blood that smeared
A diamond tapestry of gray and brown
On a body thick as my arm—
Torn where the wheel had passed.
There were thirteen rattles and a button.

Surrounding in the dust
I saw the marks he'd made—
Ridges of loops and whorls,
A massive thumbprint—
A graceful calligraphy
Of accidental beauty
Written in thwarted escape
Or reptile agony.

With fading strength
He'd pulled himself
Into the formal coil
To await the final enemy.

Alkali

They say that *alqili*
Is Arabic for wood ash
And denotes hydroxide and carbonate
Salts of sodium and potassium—
And while I've seen small branches
Of shad scale, scrub oak and juniper
Burned to fine white ash
That kept the shrunken form of twigs
Until disturbed into powder,
I cannot say it's true.

I know alkali only
As the blanched coat
That covers low ground
That has no streams,
But only flat dry lake beds
With hard, bitter soil
Supporting scattered sagebrush
And the poisonous weed halogeton.
Somehow it's not like soil at all—
Its more like salt or quicklime
That makes a white runway
Between the sage for pale jackrabbits.

Desert

The young rattler flows through sparse grass—
Head raised, black tongue feeling for sound.
But all is quiet until my boots shuffle in the dust
Then he flows faster and tapers away.

This is his world, not mine—nor any man's, though
You can see wagon tracks more than a century old.
Most crossed quickly as they could,
When the sand burned their soles.

Some thought this much land must have a use
Or constitute a dream. They left ruins
Of stone way stations at rare springs
And dark prospectors' holes in outcrops.

The valleys are twenty miles wide,
And no one is in them—you could see them,
Even the slow movement of a fool on foot—
A distant pickup trails a wedge of white dust.

A world too terrible for man to remain—
Too dry, too empty, too devoid of green—
Only blue and gray, purple, dull brown,
And pale colors that have no name.

Dale la Vuelta
(Dally)

You watch a roper at the rodeo.
He seems to drop a loop
As soon as the calf clears the chute.

His horse is a trained marvel
That sits back and snaps the rope
And flips the calf.

The roper sprints
And throws the calf again
As the rules require.

The horse keeps the tension.
And the roper wraps three legs
With the pigging string,

Then throws his hands
Up in the air
To stop the clock.

It's all rehearsed and stylized—
Like a dance—with only tenths
Of a second between top contenders.

The graded arena,
Has no rocks or brush,
And the calves are all of a size.

I guess it must be so—
For fairness sake
And money on the win.

There are crowds and flags,
Loudspeakers and clowns,
But I miss the unpredictables—

The outsize calf,
The loose cinch,
The half-broke horse.

And I miss the dust,
The morning haze
And steaming horses,

The smell of coffee
And the stench
Of the branding iron.

And I miss McClovio—
Still a stubborn dally roper—
With his three-fingered hand.

Note

Ropers are of two kinds. *Tie ropers* tie the end of the lariat to the
saddle horn. The less commonly seen *dally ropers* first catch the calf and then
make dallies—from the Spanish *dale la vuelta:* to make a loop—around the
horn. These loops with a calf on the end of the rope can catch a hand.

Single-Action Colt

Colt's called it Model P or "Peacemaker"
And Army Model '73 (in calibre .45—
Quaintly using the British spelling).
But in .44-40, they stamped the barrel—
Colorfully: "Frontier Six-Shooter"—

A shrewd marketing ploy—using
The cartridge of Winchester's '73,
"The Gun That Won the West"—
Handy to have a pistol and
Rifle use the same ammunition.

Its owners called it—with pseudo-
Deprecation, "Plowhandle," "Thumbuster,"
"Hogleg," and "Equalizer"—quoting:

> Be not afraid of any man
> No matter what his size
> If danger threatens call on me
> And I will equalize.

Colt's first gun designed for
Newfangled cartridges—and made
In calibers from .22 to .476 Eley
And barrel lengths from 3 inch
(Storekeeper's Model with no ejector rod)
To those special-order 12-inch monsters
Ned Buntline gave to Masterson and Earp.

The competition—Smith & Wesson, Starr—
Somehow lacked the lines and balance.
With blue cylinder and barrel
And color-case-hardened frame,
It was a handsome gun,
And it looked like what it was.

You could stick it in your belt
With the loading gate open
To keep it from slipping
Down in your pants.
Or carry it in a holster,
But it was rarely carried low
And tied down—Hollywood fashion.
It was a strong shooter,
But had fragile innards—
Some called it the gunsmith's friend.
Hand springs and triggers broke,
And safety notches on the hammer—
If you fanned it
Without tying the trigger back.

But it was the proper pistol,
And as an epitaph said:

> He died a violent death.
> He was shot by a Colt's revolver,
> Old kind, brass-mounted,
> And of such is the Kingdom of Heaven.

Note

The slightly odd form of *Colt's* reflects the company's formal title of
Colt's Patent Firearms.

Reno-Bentine Site

I'd read accounts of Custer—
How he had courage
But no other noticeable virtues.
It made a moral tale—
A proper comeuppance
For white man's arrogance.

And I traced the route he took—
As close as blacktop would allow
From Fort Abraham Lincoln in Dakota—
On his punitive expedition
To make the Black Hills safe
For proper gold seekers.

I came to the hills above
The Little Bighorn before daylight
On a clear summer morning.
And passed the scattered stones
That mark where Armstrong—
As George was called by family—
And his younger brother Tom—
A hero in his own right,
With two Medals of Honor—
And the others went down—
Outnumbered, outgunned,
And outgeneraled, too—
Shot, and then butchered
By squaws' skinning knives.

On the hill beyond, Reno and Bentine,
With other companies of the Seventh,
Waited that hot June afternoon.
They saw dust and heard shots and knew
They were too late and too few
To mount a saving charge.
And fearing for their own hair
Dug rifle pits around the hilltop
And waited for the dark.

The dark was safe because
Indians who died in the dark,
Went to a dark hunting ground—
Or so it was said, but you never knew,
So the night was long.
I too waited for sunup—looking down
On Little Bighorn Coulee.
The willows along the winding creek
The only green against the pale grass.

There are washes and draws
Leading up from the river—
A thousand places of concealment
Just out of rifle range—
And the memory of shots and dust
And distant yells yesterday afternoon.

And five thousand Sioux and Crow
And Cheyenne led by Sitting Bull,
Crazy Horse, and Gaul waiting
For just the right moment, and
Trapdoor Springfields reload slow.
The light came late.

It's a fearsome place to be
Alone at summer dawn.

Alfalfa

Green shoots grow from stubble
After the snow has gone—
Round stems with a groove
And staggered oval leaves.

By June they are topped with
Lavender blooms and ready to cut.
The horse-drawn mower clatters
Round and round the field—
Each swath reducing the uncut square—
Driving pheasants to the center,
Until they hide in a patch
The size of a living room.

The driver can then dismount
And flush them out by walking through,
Or keep on cutting to the end.
Some birds will fly before the blade
When there is nowhere else to hide—
Exploding upward, cackling as they climb,
Sometimes dangling a useless leg
If they wait too long.

The panicked or more conservative
Will flop headless behind the cutter—
Like axed chickens in the barnyard—
And will roast for supper.

But back to the harvest.
The man then windrows the hay
With a one-horse rake—
Up and down the field,
Taking care to trip the tines
At just the proper moment
So the windrows make straight bars.
Then he comes back another way
To rake the windrows into cocks—
Sized for one forkful each.

There they lie for days to dry—
Deep green fades in the sun—
The farmer wraps a stem around
His finger to test the moisture—
When too wet, hay mildews in the stack
Or heats up and burns the barn.

One man can cut and rake,
But loading takes a group.
They wait until the dew has gone
Then parade beside the rack,
Holding four-tined forks like spearmen
Beside the king's chariot.

A young boy drives the team.
The horses know the drill:
Pull fifty feet then wait
As men fork piles onto the rack,
Then pull ahead and wait again.

The pitchers stab their forks into
The cocks in just the proper place—
Two-thirds of the way across—
Then lift with the left hand,
Pushing down with the right—
Arms straight, then a quick hoist
That puts the cock overhead
To carry balanced to the rack
And throw on top
For the loader to arrange.

It's done with strength and grace
And not a little pride,
But with a touch of caution, too—
Rattlesnakes hide in cocks
And fall across the necks
Of pitchers and loaders
And change the working rhythm
With sudden yells and
Jumps, hayfork stabs—
And finally laughter.

The full rack drives away,
Another comes, and a boy brings
Well water in a bucket
So all can drink
Before loading up again.

The last load is scarcely gone
Before the irrigating stream
Is turned into the field—
Mountain water from the creek,
Through highline canal to cross ditch
And finally to this field
To do its replenishing.

They spread the water out with dams
Making it go as far as they can,
But there is never quite enough.
Sometimes they lose the stream and
Find it running down a gopher hole
To reappear in an inappropriate place.

Alfalfa, like its name, starts again.
A second crop will grow and bloom,
With less thistle, burdock and
Milkweed than the first.
The stalks are straighter
And have more leaves
And are all the same height.

They cut it, rake it, dry it
And haul it, the same as the first,
But stack it separate—
Second crop is said to be the best
And if sold commands a premium price.

A third crop follows
But grows more slowly—
On the down side of the solstice,
When rain comes rarely
And irrigation dwindles.

There may be a fourth after the equinox,
But on this place more often not.
At any rate they feed it to the stock
And hope it lasts the winter.

That is how it's supposed to go,
But I have rarely gotten a fourth crop—
Sometimes not a third,
And the second is not always full.
The heat and rain are often wrong,
Legs and wagons break, and snakes bite—

All crops I've known are chancy,
And some are worse than alfalfa.

Pastoral

Bright spring water
Floods the lower meadow,
Where four bay horses
Graze in the tall grass.

Lombardy Poplars

They lined both sides of streets
  In older Utah towns
    And bordered close-in fields—
      Planted close as fence posts—
        But alien to the West as settlers.

Thick-ribbed trunks and heart-shaped leaves
  Marked them kin to native cottonwoods,
    But with that peculiar spirelike form
      That spaced so close quickly
        Made a hedge fifty feet tall.

It was always said that poplars
  Were planted as windbreaks.
    And true, the sweep of wind
      Through barren basin valleys
        Could do with some impediment.

But was it that the Eastern men
  Emerging from their forest groves
    That ever blocked the distant view
      Found the scale just too immense
        And needed walls against the space.

Hermitage

It was thirty miles from town
In what we call west desert—
That empty space between the
Wasatch front and the Nevada line.

We'd heard about the place—
Follow the dirt road over the pass.
On the west side, near the bottom,
There's a narrow canyon on the right
And a car track through the sage.

You'll see an old car body—
A Buick touring car, I think,
The hermit used to drive
To town to buy supplies.

They knew him at the store
But not his name—
A lean man who didn't talk
But bought canned tomatoes
And .30-30 cartridges
With cash from coyote bounties.

He used to mail packages—
Heavy like rocks—some said
Trilobite fossils for the college,
Others said ore samples for assay—
The postmaster wouldn't tell.

There was speculation
About gold, but no one saw it—
They talked of following him
To see if he had a mine,

But that seemed unlikely.
Folks respected his privacy—and
His coyotes were shot in the head.

That was fifty years ago,
Before the war, I think,
And then he was gone—
Just gone—that's all.

When we were sure, we went out—
The canyon's narrow,
You'd miss it if you didn't know.

Big granite rocks on the sides
Like those in old cowboy movies.
Somehow it's cooler there,

And in the shade, junipers
You'd not expect in these bare hills,
Further up the canyon, piñons,
Shad scale and scrub mahogany.

He'd lived under an outcrop,
Closed in with mudchinked rocks
Like those Anasazi places.

He had a kind of stove
Made from an oil drum,
A stool cut from a cedar stump,
A table from a packing crate,
And a cupboard from a dynamite box.

Under other outcrops
He'd kept chickens and a goat.

Up the canyon, a dam below
A spring watered a garden
Of corn and beans and squash—
Like the Indians grew—
Early crops that could make
Before the stream dwindled
In rainless summer.

We'd seen deserted towns
Where hope died
When a bright vein ran out
Or the railroad took another route.
There, they can trace potentials,
And cause and effect—
Those cycles of civilization.
But this fit no historian's laws.

We talked of anchorites,
World pain, and non-herd men,
The challenge of independence,
And unrequited love.

We asked,
What kind of man . . . ?
Then let it go,
And went back to town.

The School of the Horse

My father schooled me with horses
And taught me the things
A horseman must do by habit
Without remembering he's learned.

But I recall half a century ago
How he taught me to approach horses
Slowly, with one hand slightly raised
Palm forward, fingers together
And talking low and steady
Reassuring words in horse,
"Easy *caballo,* steady fella,"

Then putting a hand on his neck
And petting him gently
While slipping a rope around.

He showed me how to put a thumb
In the corner of the mouth
Of the stubborn ones
To get them to take the bit.

Currying and brushing was
Grooming but petting, too.
And in the ritual of saddling,
He put the blanket a tad forward
And then pulled it back
To smooth down the hair.

He'd put the right stirrup
Over the saddle horn
So the saddle swung on gently.

When tightening the cinch,
He'd bump the chest with a knee
To make him blow out his puffing
So the cinch stayed snug—
Then he'd lead him a few steps
Before getting on—
In case the cinch was pinching.

"Horses," he'd say "are strong
And fast and beautiful,
But not always bright."

"They worry about their legs
And don't like surprises—
They panic easy
And like routine."

But horses and men
Were made to go together—
That's why a horse's withers
Fit a man's crotch.

Flood

How could there be water enough
To fill the cracks in playa lakes,
Water enough to saturate the sand,
To soak the gray leaves
Of sagebrush and shad scale,
To seep into the dry bark
Of juniper and Joshua.
Rain enough to soak the backs
Of mule deer and antelope.
Rain enough to drown
The horned toad and rattlesnake.
Water to fill up badger holes
And cover the cheat grass.
Rain to fill a valley thirty miles wide.
Water to lap the scrub oak
On the rocky hogsback and ripple
Against the groves of aspen
Until it reached and overspread
The pines themselves—
Black and pointed tops
Below cold waves—
Until the peaks vanished too.

No, old Noah must have launched
His ark of gopher wood
Upon a shimmering mirage.
There couldn't be that much water
In the whole dry and dusty world,
No matter how much sin.

Pioneer Graveyard

This is not the new cemetery on the hill
With flush markers the mower
Can roll over without pause
In perpetual care.
Here there are unfashionable lilacs,
Blue spruce, dogwood and wild roses.

Few of the living remember the faces
Of those buried here.
But they are names in long books
Shown by proud descendants.

Here they are marked by sandstone
Cut with more sincerity than art—
Names out of the past:
Artha, Ezekiel, Serepta, Preserved—
And inscriptions:
"Cavalry Private, Territorial Militia
During the Indian Wars."
"His toils are past, his work is done."
"She's gone but not forgotten."
"Death is but another birth."
"Planted on earth to bloom in Heaven."
Not all the words are readable—
Sandstone weathers badly.

The name on the gate says Evergreen—
A hopeful denial
Of surrounding deciduous life.

Cattle Guards

Roads and fences are incompatible.
And so there came gates.

But gates are tedious:
There is the stopping and getting out
And opening the gate and driving through,
Then stopping and getting out again
And going back to close the gate
So cattle do not follow.

Thus there came cattle guards—
A pit in the gate place,
With a dozen railroad rails over the top
So cars can rattle across.
But cattle, intimidated by the hole,
Stay in their fields.

I've never seen a steer test one.
Perhaps some Hereford Prometheus
Tried it once, and his fall
Is part of race memory,
Or bovine folklore,
But they always seem to know
Like the summer-foaled colt
Knows to break the winter pond
Ice with his hooves.

There's no Edison of cattle guards
Whose patents are infringed by copying.
Pure cattle guard design is empirical:
I doubt that anyone set the width
By calculating the standing broad jump
Of the average Holstein.

And how deep must it be to scare?
I remember making one with a pit
Four feet deep, with concrete walls—
But that was a government job,
And perhaps it was meant to allow
For filling with drifting sand.

Of late I've seen symbolic cattle guards
That are only white stripes on asphalt.
But they seem to fool the cows—
Who, after all, are not very bright.

But then I've seen men cowed
By rules and laws and commandments
Where there is no pit.

The Window

Behind the curtain
Of the open window
She stands quiet—
Eyes averted, head bowed.

She turns to peep,
Then snaps back
At the sound of kicks
And high neighs.

There were father's words,
"It's not fit a girl watch."
But more than his words,
She fears forbidden things.

While mother lived,
There were games
In the front parlor
At times like this.

Now at sixteen, she's
Woman of this house,
And likely soon,
Woman of another.

She slams the sash against
The neighs and thuds of kicks,
But most of all, the shouts
And men's coarse laughter.

Of Barns

I've seen those Eastern barns with gambrel roofs
And trim that's white against red-stained boards—
Crowned by dovecotes, cupolas and weathercocks.
They ornament the fertile farms of Ohio and Pennsylvania—
Attesting permanence, pride and prosperity.

They're not much like the barns I knew
In Sanpete, Tooele, and Parowan.
Those barns were framed with big pine poles,
Still round and with the bark left on.
The siding was rough-sawn boards
Nailed up green and left to shrink
So cracks were wide enough
To let the sparrows fly on through.

The steep-pitched roofs were only boards
Laid up and down with no shingles over.
Their edges curled toward the sun,
Making each a trough;
No matter there were gaps between—
It didn't rain much anyhow.

Nor was there ever any paint for barns;
They'd weather gray in just one year
And were ever after of indeterminate age
And nearly lost the mark of man—
Like cottonwoods, sage and sandstone bluffs.

Hotblood

What a horse Medio could have been—
Sixteen hands, eleven fifty
And grandson of Man-o-War
On his father's side—
Red sorrel with two white feet
And a star,
A coat as fine as mouse fur
that rippled over thoroughbred lean.

Foaled in Montana as a remount—
Rough-broke at three
Then turned out to grass
When the cavalry quit buying.

He was five when he came to me—
Gaunt from the railroad car
And hotblood wild—more untamable
Than any desert-caught mustang.

I was sixteen
And thought I knew my horses
From a Welsh pony
And a Morgan-Hambletonian cross.
I knew about gentling them down
With grain and curry comb
And snubbing to a tame horse
And riding on plowed ground
And holding their heads up
So they couldn't buck.

But it wasn't enough.

I lost count of the times
He pulled the *mecate* free
And threw me off.

And he ran away with me—
Two miles on a paved road,
Running like the leader in a race—
Paying no attention
To my seesawing the reins—
Until stopped before a brick wall.

Once we put him in a chute
To check his feet
And he kicked at one of us
And ripped his velvet hide
On a projecting nail.
Frantic then, he kicked again
And again and again—
Until the leg was ruined,
And he had to be destroyed.

I've known men like that.

Cottonwoods

A cottonwood on the south side
That shades an adobe wall
Can make an arid summer bearable—
As well as any modern means.

The Spaniards knew them
And called them *alamos,*
But they're unfashionable now—
And planners won't approve them.

Their roots can buckle sidewalks
And probe the water pipes.
The cotton from the female trees
Frosts the ground with lint in spring.

The males spread the walks
With catkins that stick to soles.
In fall the crop of yellow leaves
Can wear a hardy raker out.

But those are superficial things—
The planners don't like the size.
They're scaled to mesas and mountains
Not demiurban bungalows.

Their place is on the course
Of desert streams that flow
A week or two a year—
Enduring heat and cyclic drought.

They put their roots down deep
Where there's any hope of water.
It's said there's more tree
Beneath the ground than above.

They were here before the settlers
And don't seem tame—like crows
And coyotes and those hardened men
That don't look good in town.

Downhill

I sat on a rock
Below the last of sunlight on the ridge
And watched the canyon fill with dark.
The west- and north-slope pines went black;
Bats fluttered erratic flights in the dusk.
A horned owl called, another answered.
Mingled with the smell of pines
Came the faint odor of skunk.

One patch of dry June-grass showed between
Darker shapes of oak scrub and maple.
The only clear line: the sharp silhouette
Of ridge against the moonless sky.

It was time to go.
I took out my light,
Then put it back—
Deciding to walk the three miles
Down to the road without it.

I didn't know this side canyon well,
But had known others like it,
Afoot and horseback,
Day and night, in dust and snow.

I let my feet find the way—
Brushing through grass,
Sloughing over dry soil,
Making a squeaking rattle
Where the trail crossed talus.

I sensed a tree ahead and knew
The trail would go left this time
Or here would cross
The dry stream bed
And skirt the slope a ways
Before crossing back
At the next spur.

I did not stumble
Or bump my way
But walked at hiking pace
And felt secure.
The rocks and soil
And trees were part of me.

At last I heard the main-canyon creek,
And felt the ground leveling.
A short way then, and I would walk
The flat black road where men need eyes.

Grasshoppers

I walked a yellow field an August day
In bright and arid heat
That sucked the moisture from the skin
And stilled the birds—
Deterring every motion of any living thing
But grasshoppers.

They buzzed and snicked their wings
And rose in waves ahead and popped
Like corn in a heated pan.

I crossed my field again
In the low sun of January
Through blue and crusted snow
That covered up the stubble
But shrunk from sunflower stalks,
Attesting last week's thaw.

On nearly every stalk
A grasshopper—a husk
With dry dead legs that wrapped
Around the flower base—
There since some October night
When seeking a reprieve
From autumn cold,
It climbed the highest thing
And clung to plant and life—
Like an old man gripping
Rocker arms or property
Or office to ward off coming frost.

I Find Green

I find green in the gray leaves of sagebrush
Tipped with new yellow growth in April,
And green in the olive needles of juniper
Against the gray of shaley hillsides.

I find green in the leathery ears
Of prickly pear against the desert dust,
And green in the dark pines
In hollows of high north slopes.

There is green in the pale round leaves
Of aspen against white trunks
And in the yellow daffodil whose leaves
Are green spears though late snow.

And when red sandstone cliffs
Assault the eyes all day with treelessness,
I've seen the light green leaves of tamarisk
Along the river bottom burn bright green.

In a land of taupe hills, mauve mountains
And cobalt sky—with the flats below
In khaki gray and putty tan—
My eyes can still find green:

Not the universal chlorophyll
Blanketing arable earth,
But rare as an emerald
Where living things are few.

Humboldt

That saddle was new russet leather,
And it creaked when you got on.
Now it's quiet and almost black,
And the skirts and stirrup fenders
Lie flat like armadillo plates.
The basket stamp still shows in corners,
But it's mostly smooth, except for scuffs
From horns and rollovers.

That bit was blue steel
With bright silver mounts.
Now it's the brown of polished rust,
And the silver hardly shows—
Old Bally smoothed the roller,
Playing it on his tongue.

And Bally was a spraddle-legged colt
That became a high stepper
With arched neck and switching tail.
Then for a long time
He was solid and dependable.
Now he wanders the north field
In the late fall.

The kids came along and rode—
The older one cocky—
Climbing on quick,
Then sitting in the dust.

The young one—scared,
But he held on for six jumps
And that was enough.

They learned to throw a loop
And usually outsmart a cow,
But they've ridden off.

The barn I helped Dad build
Fell down last winter.
Neighbors moved in closer—
There are new fences
And shorter grass.

It's all like the streams
That rattle down the mountains,
Then roil into the Humboldt.

For a ways the river
Sparkles with promise
In the afternoon sun—

Then like a dream,
It dwindles
In the desert sand.

Wire Cut Liniment

Horses aren't bright about barbed wire.
Oh they learn to stop before a strand—
If it's stretched where they can see it.
But when it's loose and on the ground,
They can bumble into it bad.
And then they go crazy
And kick and thrash and try to run,
And gash their hocks and fetlocks.

If the horse survives his foolishness,
He will need some doctoring,
But he's often an uncooperative patient.

He won't stand still for swabbing,
And dressings don't stick to hair.
Still there's infection
And flyblow to worry about.
And the scabs that form are thick
And usually in the joints,
So they crack and open up
And slow the healing
And leave bad scars.

In such cases a proper medication
Is one part carbolic acid,
A potent antiseptic—
Two parts turpentine,
To chase away the flies—
And three parts olive oil,
To keep the scabs from cracking.

Horses don't care much for it
And more or less object.
So you squirt it on from
A distance—safe from kicks.

The formula may not be perfect,
But, it's saved horses from crippling.

Men too get tangled up with barbed wire
Of politics, religion, whiskey, women—
And other dangerous things.
They kick and run and hurt themselves,
And need medication they don't want.
For them I suggest the formula:
One part carbolic acid,
Two parts turpentine,
And three parts olive oil.

Tracks

No one saw it, but after
We read the tracks in the snow,
We knew what must have happened.

He'd left on a gray and balky horse.
A day later we followed his tracks
For ten miles or more
On barren flat through hoof-deep snow
That showed a shuffling gait,
Avoiding occasional sage,
Trotting sometimes, as if spurred,
Then dragging back to a walk
And tender on the off hind foot
Where he'd lost a shoe.

Then he'd jumped—perhaps when spurred.
Perhaps the rider's hands were deep
In sheepskin pockets hunting warmth,
Because we found where he fell
Then got up, favoring a leg—
The left I remember—
The rifle must have fallen
On the next jump.
We saw where it had landed
And been picked up.

The man's dragging trail
Led to the horse's tracks.
The horse had stopped and turned to watch
Then trotted off and stopped again.
The limping gait approached,
And again the horse trotted off—
Two thin lines in the snow
To the left of his track showed
He'd held his head to the side
To keep from stepping on the reins.

It went that way for miles—
The man's steps getting shorter
With marks beside of the rifle butt
Now used as a cane.

Then we found a cartridge case
And another and another
And the mound of a horse.
Snug against his belly was the man—
He had tried to save
What diminishing warmth remained,
But even with the saddle blanket
It hadn't been enough
For a winter night.

We talked of the judgment of fools
And wondered how we'd have done.

Reversion

My father was born in the mountains of Mexico.
On his fifth birthday in El Paso, Texas—
That was nineteen ought four—
He saw his first automobile
And got his first pair of shoes.

At thirteen he drove a six-horse span
To break one hundred and sixty acres
Of Alberta prairie grass for wheat,
Then moved to a college town
With his newly widowed mother
And became a town schoolboy—and spent
His summers breaking horses in Montana.

In college he studied agriculture, and
Played guard in the first football game he ever saw.
He taught school and coached—
And chased mustangs on the desert on weekends.

He became an administrator
Running schools with large budgets—
And had a field of black Angus cattle.

At eighty he still sat a horse well on his daily ride
And spoke of the problems and opportunities of youth.
He preached hard work and fiscal responsibility—
And the necessity of checking the cinch
Before you put your foot in the stirrup.

An Age of
Wonders

An Age of Wonders

In those days there were marvels, and I saw them:
The lombardy poplars along the street
That were even-spaced and all the same size;
The hollyhocks that made into ladies in petal gowns;
The six-sided tiles in the barbershop floor
That lay in straight rows in every direction;
The magic of a lever and a sieve and a siphon
The horse-drawn wagons of gravel that dumped
By turning the floor boards on edge
So the gravel sifted through;
Sam Lee, the blacksmith, could shape
Red iron on an anvil with a hammer;
Seeds in apricot pits tasted like almonds;
And baby rabbits were born without hair.

A horse could scratch his back by rolling over
And show he was old enough to ride;
Pine boards had a grain and could be split
Along their length but not across;
A dog's nose was cold, a cow's nose wet,
And a horse's nose was velvet;
Wood shavings curled
As they came from the plane;
A bicycle rim without its spokes
Lost all its strength;
Frost patterns on windows grew like fern leaves;
And I could bend a bar of plumber's lead
With my bare hands.

Dandelion puffs exploded into parachutes,
And maple seeds made autogiros.
The striders that skated on the water
Sank when I added soap.
Bert Weight could scribe a line
Across a piece of glass
Then break it absolutely straight;
And old Erb Matson could whistle two notes at once.

And thus I learned how the world was made
In forms and laws, results and beauty
From what the wonders were.

Curiosity

God distributed gifts.
To some he gave strength.
Others he made handsome
Or swift or let sing
Like larks at daybreak.

A last little boy asked,
Is there something for me?
God handed down an ivory box.

The boy saw the lid was curiously
Carved in a cryptic design—
It would bear some later study.
The hinges were ingeniously
Wrought, and the latch moved
With a satisfying click,
But there was nothing inside.

He stroked the surface
And looked up inquiringly.

You will have to fill it, God said
With bright pebbles and sea shells,
Maple leaves and June bugs
And red-shafted feathers.

It's a pretty thing—
I hope you find it much too small.

Smithy

Eisenhower, Ferrara, Lefevre,
Kowalski, Herrera and Toliver:
The many names for Smith—
The maker with iron.

The names remain when blacksmiths
And farriers have gone the way
Of draft horses and Conestoga wagons—
Vocational appellations like
Glover or Slater or Wheelwright—
Common and current in every tongue.

Were there more smiths than tailors?
There must have been more farmers!
Were they more prolific
Than carpenters or thatchers?
Or did the names persist because
They caught the magic of the forge?

It must be that—the heating iron
In a forge with coke or charcoal,
With a manmade wind of bellows blast.

And magic it is, when the black iron,
Buried deep in coals turns cherry red—
That is how it's said—

Between the red and black
An indescribable shade of infrared,
And on the edges, darker flakes
Against the brighter inner core.

Then upon the solid anvil face
It's beaten on and formed—
Like many things.

You watch the hammer rise
And fall, and hear the clang—
A hard blow,
Then a light one
To mark the place.
The first dull strikes,
Like hitting slushy ice,
But as the redness fades
The tones ring up the scale,
Like water bubbling up a bottle.

With measured blows, the smith
Can make a round bar flat
Or make a flat bar round—
He has a pile of swages
For shaping other forms.
And when the hammering's done,
He thrusts the iron in the water
In a barrel—the flash of steam
Makes a hole around the iron—
The rushing hiss goes down in tone
And ends in pops and bubbles.

Long before metallurgy and talk
Of grain size and names
Like Austenite and Martensite,
Smiths knew the black art of
Quick quench and slow quench
And temper and anneal.

So they could with heat and blows
Shape the plows and cutting blades,
The spears and swords and armor—
Makers with those other smiths
Hephaestus, Thor, and Vulcan.

The Culvert's Rise

Utah irrigation ditches
Have sovereign right of way
Sacred as the king's highway.

Thus Main Street accommodated—
For its hundred foot width—
The Settlement Canyon stream
With an elegant culvert.

But long culverts clog
With leaves and branches,
Apples and kids' boats.
They require poles
And fire hoses to clear.

For access this one was roofed
With cast-iron plates
So heavy the end of one
Was all a man cared to lift.

One hot night a coffee can of carbide
Floated into the culvert—
In its bottom a metered nail hole
That let it sink halfway through.

Carbide and water produce acetylene—
A smelly flammable gas.

From half a block away another can
Floated down, with a lighted oily rag—
Like a fire ship under full sail
Into the anchored frigates at Brest.

Blue flames squirted, riding a dull boom
And the heavy clang of plates
Lifted and fallen awry.

It was glorious and satisfying.
Investigators could not find the cause,
Though there was talk of sewer gas.
The miscreants were never caught—
And there is the statute of limitations.

My Earliest Memory

I know I was younger than three
When I tried to hold back
An invasion of red ants.

I don't recall being
Detailed to the mission,
But I took it seriously
And sat on the sidewalk,
Legs spread, swinging
My father's green-handled hammer
With both hands, trying
To hit scurrying ants.

No one kept a body count,
But I am sure I slew battalions.
Slaughter was tiring work
Beneath the summer sun.

Most of all I remember
The infiltrators
Crawling though my clothes.
And I could feel them on
The soft skin of my neck
And tried to squeeze them
By lowering my chin.

That thin neck skin
Is a tender place to bite.
And thus I early learned
About retribution—
And the balance of Nature.

Excavation

The boy kneels at the mound of soil
Left from digging a trench.
He excavates roads to the summit
For his toy trucks,
Digging with a shovel
Whittled from a cedar shingle.
But thwarted by the dryness of the dirt—
Too powdery to pack into walls,
Or hold the bank of a dugway,
Or make a proper tunnel
Like the good damp dirt down deep—
He scrapes away the surface,
Repeating the desert child's litany:
Dry dirt, you go away,
Wet dirt, you come here.
Dry dirt, you go away,
Wet dirt, you come here.

Warren Piece

My father was no architect of public halls
Or carpenter of stately homes,
But he built fine rabbit pens—
That is he directed me in their carpentry.
I built enough for an urban warren—
At least, if he'd saved them all.

But someone would come by
And admire his stock—
Praising pink eyes and white fur
And the delicacy of upright ears.
In a burst of generosity
He'd offer a start—
Like a start of sourdough or buttermilk—
And so he'd give a buck
And a pair of does
With an empty nail keg for a nest box;
It was always the same.
The new husbandman would,
Of course, need a pen,
And last year's creation
Would be trundled off,
Leaving only the newest one
Standing alone—inadequate
For rabbit fecundity.

I've wondered since at father's motives,
If it all was generosity—
Or just the chance to build a pen
(Or have one built)
A little better than the last.

There were changes always—
An improvement in the feeder,
And three tiers instead of two,
Or a subtle alteration in the
Angle of the slanted floor—
As he pursued through ascending forms
Some Platonic ideal
Of the ultimate rabbit pen—
Warm enough in winter,
Cool enough in summer,
But above all, self-cleaning.

He might have had that ivory hutch,
Had he not had some strain
Of Puritan penury that barred
New boards or screen or nails.
So every pen was a palimpsest,
With weather-checked boards,
New-cut on the ends,
And rust-ringed holes
Where nails had been
In an earlier avatar.

The nails themselves,
Carefully pulled—with broken heads—
Were pounded fairly straight
Then driven in again.

Those ideal pens grew
More grand in concept,
But depleting stocks
Of screen and boards
Made each execution poorer,
And so it balanced out.

I have not shaken yet
The ghost of building rabbit pens.
The years have passed,
And I conceive more grandly now,
But I take my stock
From a depleting pile.

Muska and the Porcupines

Muska was a serious dog.
Big for a springer
And not full feathered
Like a pampered show dog.
His coat was short and scraggly—
Despite his champion pedigree.
His ears were full of cockleburs,
As befits a hunter.

He would retrieve ducks and geese
From the coldest water and smell out
Pheasants and flush them—
Sometimes breaking protocol of the hunt
And catching them in the tules—
Carrying them back fluttering,
With as much pride as if
They'd fallen to the gun.
And he'd hunt for anyone—
Unless they missed too often.

Bird season doesn't last long,
But the horses were ridden year round,
So he'd follow to run and hunt—
Killing cottontails and chasing deer.
You'd hear him cross the ridge,
Baying like a coon hound, with a hook
On his bark you could hang a bucket on.

We could not break him of killing
Chickens—and sometimes cats.
And he stunk—not just wet-dog odor
Like scalded chicken feathers,
But he carried a lingering odor of skunk
That tomato juice would not wash out
And the rancid stench of rolled-in carrion.

He was hit by a car—and a truck—
And three times kicked by horses.
And he'd fight when challenged—
A bad mauling by a big Alsatian
Didn't deter him the next encounter.

And he attacked porcupines.
He'd come home with a muzzlefull
Of quills, like some odd beard—
The white ends out and black barbs
Buried in nose and lips and gums,
And some clean through his tongue.
These were not from a slap of tail—
It was plain he'd tried to bite.

It took an hour's work
With pliers to pull them out,
While he struggled to be patient.
But he yelped and sometimes snapped.
The quills are hollow,
And they say if you snip the ends,
They deflate and come out easier.
But it didn't seem to help.

You'd think he'd learn from that.
But in a while he'd be stuck again.
What a damfool dog, but then,
I'm not sure I'm smarter.

The World of Men

The World of Men

He was just a little boy,
And his right eye was crossed,
So he squinted it and looked
At the world through the other one.
His hair was like dandelion seed,
And his father's friends would tease,
"Where did you get that white hair?"
And he would reply with intended precision
(for even then he was passionate about truth),
But in a voice that squeaked,
"My hair is dark white."

His father's friends always knew what to do
When a horse needed shoeing or a car broke.
There was wiry Willard McLaws, who
Could put a strap around a refrigerator
And carry it up a flight of stairs.
And Ed Gillespie, who at rodeos
Could pluck a bronc rider from the back
Of a bucking horse when the whistle blew.
And Shag Tate that his father taught him
To say was the ugliest man in town;
And Minky, who'd been All-American
Halfback and called the boy Sour Puss.

He followed his father into their world,
Watched their arm wrestling,
And listened to their talk
About quarterbacks and deer hunts
And cutting horses and Chevrolets,
And the eternal argument over whether Shag
Was really uglier than Rufus Bevan.

The boy walked a little spraddle-legged
Like his father—though he was
Knock-kneed rather than bowlegged—
And he tried to wave at people on the street
Using two fingers the way his father did.
And at night in his prayers
He said, "God bless Minky,
And Ed Gillespie, and Willard McLaws."

Forgery

The poet from himself
And his cosmos
Forges an anvil
Ironically
According to his cast
And his temper
Then grinds it hard
And files it.

Upon its polished face
He lays his reputation
And his gonads
Handing hammers out to all
Inviting them to swing
And prove his metal.

Arma Virumque Cano

Arma I
.50 Caliber Browning

In WWI Browning conceived it—
Big brother to his .30 cal—
Not artillery precisely,
But enough against early tanks
Though that war ended too soon
For action in campaign.

In War Deuce it had its chance
In wings of Mustangs and Jugs,
In turret mounts of Forts and Libs,
And in half-track quads.
It continued on in similar use
In the Korean misunderstanding.

In Nam, rockets took its place
For combat in the air.
Though it continued on the ground—
Heavy for any infantry role,
But accurate, capable
And utterly dependable.

You see it now in film clips
From the Arabian sandbox—
Firing from a HUM-V mount.
It soldiers on—
Older than any soldier there—
Almost coeval with war.

Arma II
Shaped Charge

Let me explain Monroe effect,
The principle of shaped charge.
You see this rocket's hollow nose—
The shaped charge is behind—
It has a cupped face of TNT.

When the rocket strikes,
This fuse right here
Ignites the charge, and
The blast is focused so—
Like an acetylene torch.

It bores a hole in armor plate,
Spewing molten steel around inside—
Like a BB in a basin—
Igniting fuel or ammo
And perforating enclosed EM.

Virum I
Soldiers of the Legion

To the hospital at Clark in the Philippines
They were flown from Dien Bien Phu.
Legionnaires with wound dressings three days old.
Lean, sun-browned men with shaven heads,
Ignoring pain, full of Gallic jests—
Raucous, swearing in six languages,
Making tough army nurses blush
At frank suggestions.
With my noncombat injury,
I lay half in awe, half in terror.

One, LeClerq, lay in a bed by the wall,
Quiet and alone with his lower leg gone.

Later, when they could limp
About the ward in blue pajamas,
Kowal, Huygens, Cutter and Hartmann
Broke up their noisy card game
And pounced on LeClerq.
Laughing, they held him down,
And with ceremony exposed his stump
And tickled it with a feather,
While he thrashed and raged
And swore what he would do to them
When he got back on his feet.

Virum II
Guard Mount

I always liked the ritual, son,
It gives comfort in uncertain times—
The standing tall, the cadence count—
Each man knows his place—and
You show you're one with the rest
When you do the manual of arms.

You know how you stand in ranks
And wait for the brass to step
In front and do left face
And try to make you blink
In that intimidating way
The young ones think is military.

You keep your eyes ahead
And snap your weapon
To inspection arms,
And wait for him to make
A grab to take the piece
To see if it's clean enough.

It's a kind of contest, son,
If you let go before he grabs,
The weapon falls upon the ground,
And you will sleep with that rifle
On your narrow cot until another
Trooper makes the same mistake.

But if you hold too long,
When he grabs the handguard,
The rifle butt will pivot round
And hit you in a tender place—
And the unwritten rule
Says you may not wince.
But you can watch his shoulder—
It telegraphs his move
So you can let the rifle go
At just the proper time, and
Save the comfort of your bed
And the precious family jewels.

Corporal Michael McKillip
Was the sharpest one I've seen.
He had that edge beyond correct,
With spin-buffed brass
And Corcoran boots that
Shone like a looking glass.

Once I watched him snap to,
And raise that M1 up—
Precise in every move—
Young Lieutenant Budd
Tried to stare him down,
But couldn't make him blink.

From the rank behind
I saw McKillip's thumb
Hooked in the trigger guard—
I knew his game—few men dared it—
Thumb the piece down
Faster than gravity's fall.

Budd's hand flashed, but
Quicker yet, the rifle dropped.
Budd's open palm caught
The sharp front sight.
I saw blood ooze
From gripping fingers.

Budd was young but stout.
Though his face went white,
He sharply carried on.
Young lieutenants would be wise
To pass by the rifles
Of corporals and buck sergeants.

Notes for civilians

1. The title is the opening line of Vergil's *Aeneid:* "I sing of arms and the man."

2. The .50 caliber Browning machine gun has been in continuous service since 1919. It is essentially a scaled-up version of the earlier .30 caliber Browning.

3. War Deuce is old soldiers' jargon for World War II.

4. Mustangs (P-51s) and Jugs (P-47 Thunderbolts) were World War II fighter aircraft. Forts (B-17 Flying Fortresses) and Libs (B-24 Liberators) were heavy bombers.

5. Half-track quads were quadruple .50 caliber machine guns mounted on armored trucks that had tanklike tracks in place of rear wheels.

6. HUM-V is a current-issue military vehicle resembling a jeep but much larger.

7. A shaped charge is an explosive in the nose of a rocket or artillery shell. Its shape concentrates the explosive force and allows it to penetrate thick armor.

8. EM is a military abbreviation for Enlisted Men.

9. The Legion is the famous French Foreign Legion. The Legion fought in French Indochina (which was later Vietnam) with U.S. support against Viet Cong insurgents. Their final (and losing) battle in Indochina was at Dien Bien Phu in 1954.

10. The guard-mount procedure and accompanying tradition of "thumbing down the piece" existed through the days of the M1 rifle and its successor, the M14. It probably goes back at least to the days of the Springfield. The thumbing-down tradition has apparently been lost with the current M16.

Before the Launch

We wait—
The machine on its pad,
I on mine.

The machine:
Designed for the mission precisely,
Evolved and carefully perfected
In aerodynamic form
And exotic materials—
Linear graphite, boron fiber, titanium—
And miles of pipes and wires,
With monitors for every strain and function.

But I:
I was not designed for this,
Just modified in a hundred ways to fit—
Selected, trained and wired,
Plumbed cocooned and
Put on this couch to wait—
To wait the flame and thrust
Then glorious soaring triumph—
The achievement of invention and skill—

So here I lie in unheroic posture,
Tasting the plastic tang of unnatural air,
Encumbered, anticipating multiple G's
And insults to soft tissues,
Then the floating in the dark
Like a dust mote in a sunbeam—

The machine has known some faults—
Failures to ignite,
And flights that started well
But veered off course
And had to be destroyed,

I have had miscalculations, too,
And times of indecision,
Leaden stupidity,
Clumsiness
And frozen fear—

We wait.

Note

Written when I tried to apply for the teacher-in-space program a year before the Challenger disaster.

Flight

I've envied red-tailed hawks in flight
And condors with their bowed and tilting wings—
Their primary feathers fingering banks
Into the thermal's rise.
I've seen them feel the breeze
To row and pull and drag
And sweep through depths of wind
And curves of air.

I've watched the falcon's folded plunge
And gulls hovering in offshore breeze,
And seen the snow geese
Approaching low in squalling wind
With webbed feet spread
And braking wings whistling in the rain.

I've seen the great blue heron
Lift from the shallow pond
With a single stroke of wing,
And watched with awe the rubythroat
Stand in air to stab the morning glory,
And heard the fluttering murmur
Of waxwing flocks around the pyracantha.

Instead of wings
I was born with hands
That cannot fan the empty air
And lift my heavy bones.

But I can dream of flight—
My hands have fashioned wings
That lift me to the bird's domain,
Where I look down on wrinkled hills
And geometric farms and know
What earthbound man can only dream.

I penetrate the frothy clouds
And feel the substance of the air.
I sense its hardness
And its currents with my wings.

I know my plane,
It's like myself.
I know and trust the strength
Of spars as I trust my bones.
I felt and shaped the gusseted longerons.
The glued and bradded ribs are part of me.
I feel the tension of each cable
And crimp of every sleeve and thimble—
They're like my joints and sinews.

I will my wings into a climbing turn
And feel the G's against my structure
And soar with eagle's pride
To know that flight is mine.

Disclaimer

Death, old friend,
We've met before.
I know that dour face;
Your bony beckoning hand
Signs to me a brotherhood.

But I'll remain a while,
If you'll allow.

For roads and tasks—
And words not written down.
I need not have them all,
But some are dear.

Gladly then, I'll go with you
And feel the cool enfolding
Of your robes, your gentle dark
And your soft anodyne for pain.

On Sunday

Dedication Hymn

Wanting Lord, this house of prayer,
We measured out its form with care;
Its foundation in thy ground
Laid we solidly and sound—
Built the walls of stone and brick,
Bonded firm and straight and thick—
Sill and studding, truss and plate,
Beam and rafter, sheath and slate—
Tightly fitted, plumb and true,
Workmanlike, the building through.

Sanctify this house, O Lord,
Bless each stone and brick and board;
Shield it from the curses hurled
By a broad and alien world;
Let it be a gospel school,
Teaching us thine overrule—
Place for hymn and holy praise,
Raised to thee of endless days;
Let this house be as thine own—
Thou foundation, cornerstone.

Note

"Dedication Hymn" was set to music by David Sargeant.

E. H. 1817

It looks like any framing square,
Twenty-four inches on the stock
Sixteen on the leg.
I'm told twice-great grandfather Emer
Forged it from a sword.
It bears his mark—E. H. 1817.

The numbers and the marks are faint
But readable still
When you slant it to the light
To show the dents of hammer blows.

The graduations are widespread—
No subtleties beyond a quarter inch—
But I cannot fault their accuracy
With the finest modern scale.

They say he used it in building
The temple at Nauvoo—
I wonder where his compass is—
And Brigham left him to build
A ferry for following companies
At the last crossing of the Platte.

With it he built the house
And the church at Clarkston,
And his son built at Alpine and Monroe
And his at Payson, Colonia Juarez, and Cardston
And his at Logan and Richmond and Tooele—
Scattered places on a western map,
New towns with straight streets
And square corners.

It leans by the bookshelf now—
An heirloom, a conversation piece for show.
But its angle is true—
If it were needed for building
A New Jerusalem.

Benjamin

What is it a father finds
    in one to favor over others?
Did Isaac know what grace was his
    in primogeniture,
While Ishmael wandered?

Did Esau question his father's way
    and think the pottage just
A specious way to further
    predestination—

To choose my father,
    who passed along that
Odd selection, too,
    so Joseph was his pet.

I heard him say that Rachel
    was his love,
And he saw her eyes
    in Joseph's face.

I know the ancient tales
    of brothers—
One chosen, the other not,
    inexplicably,

And like Abel's brother
    I wish I knew
Why God must choose.

The Magi

A scholar reading cryptic lines
And one who read the bowl of night
Had called the sage geometer,
Who traced the curve in solemn rite;
And thus assured, to find a child,
Three learnéd men once crossed a world.
And still men study fragile scrolls
And chart a many-layered sphere,
And still men watch the ancient stars—
Compounding knowledge year on year;
The towers of their learning grow,
As subtle scholars persevere.
   O wise men may ye ever bring
   Your gifts to lay before your king.

—in collaboration with son Steven Harris

Apprentice

While yet a boy he learned his father's trade—
Watching the scribe of the compass arc,
Standing in the sawpit with dust in his eyes,
Swinging the adze to cut to the line,
Holding the chisel tight under mallet blows
Against the crooked grain of olive wood,
Fitting the tenon close and locking it
With hammered pegs in augured holes,
Plumbing the post, leveling the beam and
Setting the latch—he mastered it all.

He left that trade to teach—
To mark the line
And hew men's lives—
Till lifted up on post and beam,
He hung upon the nails
And showed he knew his Father's trade.

At the Ziggurat

From the center they set stones
Outward and upward in a spiral
Like the shell of a snail.

Perhaps laying the whole foundation first,
But more likely starting small
And later adding outer courses
To make the progress seem more rapid—
Heaven is a long way up.

It is not clear why that objective
Should have given such offense,
But it did, they say,
And confusion came.

The Chaldean-speaking stonecutter
Ceased to comprehend the Indic
Words the mason spoke.

And only the oxen understood
The driver's Egyptic speech.

With tongues and minds perplexed
They let the tower go
And scattered to the winds.

Thus Turks and Poles
And Swedes and Thai
Are far apart
As you and I.

Son Loss

O God, who knew when Israel grieved
That Joseph had not died,
And felt the pain of Job's loss, too,
Of sons so early dead—
And Saul who wept for Jonathan
Was watched by thee, who knew—
O God, who saw that Lot left sons
In cities of the plain,
And with a ram saved Abraham
The sacrifice of son—

Gracious God, who wept with thee
When thy son died?

Cutting Loose

Three Triolets

Irrationality

We totter on the brink of sanity,
But steadied by irrational acts,
Those glitches that save humanity.
We totter on the brink of sanity.
Wisdom and reason are vanity
And blatant denial of facts.
We totter on the brink of sanity
But steadied by irrational acts.

Awakening

That love would end I should have guessed;
It always does, they tell me.
This one has been just like the rest;
That love would end I should have guessed.
I always think that I've been blessed—
What tawdry goods they sell me.
That love would end I should have guessed;
It always does, they tell me.

Romance

An April–September romance—
The fantasy of middle age.
They wonder if there's a chance
An April–September romance.
The ratchet years advance—
The calendar turns a page.
An April–September romance—
The fantasy of middle age.

To a Celibate Friend Marrying Late

I wonder how it is at last
   When well past youth,
Having withstood siege
   For more than half a life,
To succumb to love—
   Surrendering at last the citadel
Of autonomy for favorable terms.

It cannot be the randy, rutting urge
   That betrayed the others still
Wet behind the ears
   And in their playmate dreams.

But this loving rationally,
   With premeditation
After lengthy waiting,
   Like Jacob laboring his
Seven years to earn his bride—

Well, *consummatum est* and a jab
   In the ribs, and hope
For love that all men wish
   And some men know.

Two Mnemonic Odes on the Phonetic Alphabet

I. Classicism

ABLE, the
BAKER, and
CHARLIE—whose
DOG could
EASY catch a
FOX—and
GEORGE could not understand
HOW such an
ITEM got in the paper. But in
JIG time the
KING—for the
LOVE of
MIKE—ordered
NAN not to play her
OBOE. While
PETER the Great gave the
QUEEN and
ROGER
SUGAR in their tea, he could not
TARE
UNCLE
VICTOR and
WILLIAM from viewing
X-RAYs of the
YOKE on a
ZEBRA

II. Modernism

ALPHAbet soup for dinner?
BRAVO!
CHARLIE, did you see the
DELTA-winged jets
ECHO and
FOXTROT across the sky to a
GOLF
HOTEL? Last
INDIAn summer
JULIET brought me a
KILO from
LIMA, which lasted me and
MIKE clear till
NOVEMBER, when
OSCAR came to town. But
PAPA fled to
QUEBEC and
ROMEO to the
SIERRA madre to dance the
TANGO in the
UNIFORM of the
VICTOR, but a
WHISKEY-dream
X-RAY showed a
YANKEE skeleton inside the
ZULU.

Before the Written Word

Twenty five centuries ago,
Englishmen lived in caves,
And to ward off evil
Or look more fierce,
They painted themselves
With woad,
A fashionable blue.

Meanwhile, in Zululand,
Where all men are brave—
As Haggard tells—
The enterprising Zulu
Took to smelting iron.

It was a quantum leap in
Armament over the Kukuyu
And Hottentots.

Their impis charged
In serried ranks
With iron-tipped assegais
To challenge even
The towering Watusi
And formidable Masai.

Their epic battles
Might have rivaled Malden
Or Crécy, or Agincourt.
Regrettably we do not know.
They left no written tales—
Just those around the campfire told.

They built no moated castles
With cloistered libraries
For illuminated vellums.

It was quite enough, they thought,
To pass on down by word of mouth
To sons the tales of fathers' glory
And grandfathers' deeds at arms—

And some small part of
The art of making iron.

Bless Our Tacky Chapel

In subdivision you can search
For our prefabricated church—
Asphalt roofing, plywood walls,
Nylon carpet in the halls.

Bless the pulpit made of beech
With clock therein for timing speech,
And Lennox air conditioners
For cooling down parishioners.

Best Crane plumbing in the johns,
Astroturf in all the lawns.
Bless the amplifier, Lord,
Socket, plug and tangled cord—

A baby's squall of strident tone
With feedback through the microphone.
No other chapel has the class
Of molded pews of fiberglass

And classroom bells that can be rung
By buttons on the podium.
The concrete footings stand the load
According to the building code.

We'd leave the church at parting knell—
But the aluminum steeple has no bell.

Insecta

You chitinous hexapod—
You trisegmented vermin—
How dare you challenge Homo sapiens.
I have seen your munching mandibles
Mowing mindlessly.
And your probosci sucking sap and serum
Indiscriminately.
I have watched your colonies,
With their gene-mandated
Governance and obedience.
I have seen the salvage operations
On dung and carrion—
Where's the dignity in all that?

I'll not deny the Lepidoptera
Has color but little grace.
And there is a beauty of sorts
In the blue-green-black
Of certain species of Coleoptera.
And an elegant mathematics
To hexagonal brood cells in apian nests.
But this capricious metamorphosis
This egg to larva to pupa to adult—
It's clear to all
You don't know what you're about.

I dismiss your entire arthropodic tribe.
I dismiss your megamillennial genealogy.
I dismiss your endless adaptations,
Your countless evolutions,
Your acquired immunities to toxic agents.
And eating more of human food than humans do
I dismiss you as vector of disease
I dismiss your filling every biological niche
I dismiss your sucking my blood
I dismiss your eating my front porch.
I will prevail, I must!

The Published Poems of John Sterling Harris: A Bibliography

"Alkali," "Tracks," and "Grasshoppers." *BYU Studies* 24 (summer 1984): 337–40.

"The Assassination of Emma Gray" and "Hay Derrick." In *A Believing People,* ed. Richard Cracroft and Neal Lambert, 303–5. [Provo, Utah]: Brigham Young University Press, 1974. Reprint. Salt Lake City: Bookcraft, 1979.

Barbed Wire. Provo, Utah: Brigham Young University Press, 1974. Contains "First Spring Ride," "Adaptation," "Watering Turn," "Rock Pile," "Hawk," "Progress," "Polly Sleeps," "Hay Derrick," "Daddy Long Legs," "Mercur, Utah," "The Gate," "Notes on Infantry Weapons," ("M1 Rifle," "Flame Thrower," "Browning Machine Gun," ".45," "M16," "Grenade," "Rocket Launcher," "Carbine," "M3 Submachine Gun"), "Tag, I.D.," "The Whittler," "Populus Tremulus," "Fallow," "Juniper Trees," "Teleology," "Canticle Two," "Tack Room," "Hackamore," "Ice Crystals," "Vulnerability," "Incident in the Ice Cream Parlor," "Canticle One," "Horned Toad," and "The Assassination of Emma Gray."

"Benjamin." *BYU Studies* 24 (spring 1984): 150.

"Black Whole." *Teaching English in the Two-Year College* 15 (December 1988): 220.

"Canticle One." *Improvement Era* 73 (September 1970): 62.

"Canticle Two." *Improvement Era* 73 (January 1970): 29.

"Desert," "I Find Green," and "Soldiers of the Legion." *Tar River Poetry* 31, no. 1 (fall 1991): 39–41.

"Disclaimer." *BYU Studies* 32, no. 3 (1992): 46.

"E. H. 1817," "Apprentice," and "When I See Thy Strength, O Lord." In *Poems of Praise,* ed. Edward L. Hart and Marden J. Clark, 26, 27, 38. [Provo, Utah]: Brigham Young University Press, 1980.

"Excavation." *BYU Studies* 3 (summer 1987): 90.

"Fallow." *Dialogue* 7 (autumn 1972): 71–72.

"Fallow," "F. H. 1817," "Hay Derrick," "Tag, I.D.," and "Apprentice." In *Harvest: Contemporary Mormon Poems,* ed. Eugene England and Dennis Clark, 45–50. Salt Lake City: Signature Books, 1989.

"The Gate." *Wye* (spring 1971): 63.

"The Gate," "Fallow," "Hay Derrick," and "The Unhobbled Mare." In *Prose and Poetry of the American West,* ed. James C. Work, 660–68. [Omaha]: University of Nebraska Press, 1990.

"Hay Derrick," and "Tag, I.D." In *Modern Poetry of Western America: An Anthology,* ed. Clinton F. Larson and William Stafford, 171–72. [Provo, Utah]: Brigham Young University Press, 1975.

"Hay Derrick." *BYU Studies* 14 (winter 1974): 270–71.

"Hotblood." *BYU Studies* 29, no. 3 (1989): 69.

"Incident in an Ice Cream Parlor." In *Ideas of Order,* ed. Marion B. Brady and Roy K. Bird, 256. [Provo, Utah]: Brigham Young University Publications, 1976.

"Lombardy Poplars." *BYU Studies* 28, no. 3 (1988): 28.

"The Magi." With Steven Harris. *Mountainwest* 3 (December 1977): 30.

"Rabbit Pen." *Mountainwest* 1 (October 1975): 10.

"Reversion." *BYU Studies* 25 (summer 1985): 66.

"Rock Pile." *Carpenter* 1, no. 2 (summer 1969): 47–48.

"Search for Flight." *Sport Aviation* 33 (May 1984): 36.

"Tag, I.D." *BYU Studies* 6 (winter 1965): 100.

"Tag, I.D.," "M1 Rifle," "Flame Thrower," "Grenade," "Browning Machine Gun," "Carbine," "M16," ".45," and "SMG." In *Listen, the War,* ed. Frederick Kiley and Anthony Dater, 24–27. [Colorado Springs]: U.S. Air Force Academy, 1973.

"Teleology." *Improvement Era* 73 (February 1970): 27.

"The Unhobbled Mare." *Dialogue: A Journal of Mormon Thought* 3 (winter 1968): 94–95.

"The Window." *BYU Studies* 33, no. 1 (1993): 109.

"The World of Men," "Rattler," and "Age of Wonders." *BYU Studies* 30 (fall 1990): 20, 57, 69.